MESSAGES
❧ FROM THE ❧
MASTERS

MESSAGES
❧ FROM THE ❧
MASTERS

Tapping into the
Power of Love

BRIAN WEISS, M.D.

WARNER BOOKS

A Time Warner Company

Warner Books, Inc., 1271 Avenue of the Americas, New York, NY 10020
Visit our Web site at www.twbookmark.com

 A Time Warner Company

Printed in the United States of America
First Warner Books Printing: May 2000
10 9 8 7 6 5 4 3 2 1

Library of Congress Cataloging-in-Publication Data

Weiss, Brian L. (Brian Leslie).
    Messages from the masters : tapping into the power of love / Brian Weiss.
        p.   cm.
    ISBN 0-446-52596-0
    1. Love—Miscellanea.   2. Conduct of life—Miscellanea.   3. Reincarnation therapy.
I. Title.

BF1045.L7 W45 2000
131—dc21

                                                                99-049043

Book design by Giorgetta Bell McRee

Acknowledgments

My wife, Carole, is a constant source of love, support, and encouragement for me. I cannot begin to express the depth of my gratitude to her. She has made my books possible and has reminded me how extraordinarily wonderful it is to live a life with a soulmate.

My deepest appreciation goes to Joni Evans, my literary agent, who is such a great and talented person. She is a constant joy to work with.

I am also indebted to Jessica Papin and Tina Andreadis at Warner Books. Jessica is my editor, and her insights and superb literary skills have helped this book immeasurably. Tina has done a masterful job with the publicity of all my books, and her skill and gracious heart are deeply appreciated.

I want to thank Larry Kirshbaum for bringing me to Warner Books. His enthusiasm and support mean a great deal to me.

There are so many others to thank. I am grateful to all of you.

Contents

❧ CHAPTER ONE ❧

The Beginning

Our task is to learn, to become God-like through knowledge. We know so little. . . . By knowledge we approach God, and then we can rest. Then we come back to teach and help others.

For those of you meeting me for the first time, a few words of introduction are needed. I have come a long way from that fateful day when I, a classically trained physician, professor of psychiatry, and confirmed skeptic, realized that human life is grander and more profound than even my rigorous medical training had led me to believe.

Educated as an academic, I received my undergraduate degree from Columbia University and my medical degree from the Yale University School of Medicine, where I was also the chief resident in psychiatry. I have been on the teaching faculties of several university medical schools, and for eleven years I served as chairman of the Department of Psychiatry at Mount Sinai Medical Center in Miami Beach, Florida. By the time I first met Catherine, the patient whose story is told in my first book, *Many Lives, Many Masters*, I had published more than forty scientific papers and book chapters, and I had achieved international recognition in the fields of psychopharmacology and brain chemistry. Not surprisingly, I was completely skeptical of "unscientific" fields such as parapsychology. I knew nothing about the concept of past lives or reincarnation, nor did I want to.

And then came my sudden and shocking introduction to the spiritual, the "right-brain," the non-linear. Catherine inexplicably began recalling what seemed to be past-life memories. Somehow, all of her clinical symptoms improved via this regression process. I was amazed, but I was also beginning to find the harmony between science and intuition.

This process began twenty years ago. And since then I have regressed more than two thousand more patients to perinatal, in-utero, or past-life memories. I have already written three books about these experiences, and the books have been translated into nearly thirty languages.

Because my work deals with the themes of reincarnation, past-life regression therapy, and the reunion of soulmates, I have become the unofficial dean of reincarnation. I welcome this characterization, because I believe we *do* reincarnate until we learn our lessons and graduate. And, as I have repeatedly pointed out, there is considerable historical and clinical evidence that reincarnation is a reality.

But this book, which reflects what I teach my patients and audiences today, is about much more than reincarnation and regression therapy. These are important parts of the puzzle, but there are also other important pieces, and one must know them all and know them well. I have studied healers, mediums, psychics, and others involved in holistic and alternative practices, and I have learned that there are other avenues to one's spiritual awakening.

This book represents the culmination of twenty years of experience and studies, not only with reincarnation, but in the movement known as New Age. It is my attempt to remind you about love and joy and to teach you how to bring these qualities into your life *now*, while you are in physical state. You will learn techniques for achieving levels of inner peace and happiness that may be lacking in your present lives. You will find a great deal of material about the nature of the soul, about immortality, and about values. There are many practical tips and techniques for transforming your life, your relationships, your moods and mental states, your physical health and well-being, and your destiny. Knowledge of past lives is not necessary to achieve these positive changes. The ultimate key is understanding. As you understand your true nature and your true purpose, your life will be permanently transformed, and then you can begin to transform the world.

My life has been changing the same way. Past lives are still a significant concept and value for me, but understanding and experiencing and expressing love, joy, and inner peace in my everyday life have become more significant. I am extremely grateful that Catherine came into my office on that fateful day and opened my mind to the concept of past lives, as this became the avenue to my personal awakening. And this awakening led to spiritual growth and understanding.

A striking and important feature of Catherine's regressions was her ability while deeply hypnotized to channel or transmit detailed and accurate information from higher sources of knowledge. This material has been inspiring and life-transforming to many thousands of people from all over the planet. Catherine attributed the source of this wisdom to the "Masters," highly evolved souls not in physical form. They told her "wise and wonderful things," and she relayed this information to me. After emerging from the hypnotic state, Catherine could remember many details from the past lives she had just experienced, but she never remembered anything about her contact with these Masters because the messages from the Masters were transmitted *through* her and did not originate *from* her memory.

In letters and at speaking engagements, I am regularly besieged with requests for more messages from the Masters.

"Have you heard more?"

"Are you still in contact with them?"

"What more have you learned?"

The answer is yes. The answer is this book. Through other patients, my travels, and my own meditation, I have learned so much more.

In addition, it has become clear that we need to understand at a deeper level what has already been provided. Thus, key messages from my earlier books have been partially reproduced here, in italics, at the beginning of each chapter and sometimes within the chapter.

In knitting together the old and the new, I have become aware that an entire spiritual philosophy has been gently unfolded and handed to me. At its center is love. I believe that we, as humans, are ready to embrace it.

Especially over the past thirty years, we have been searching for stability by reviving ancient wisdom, as if the sheer volume of our scientific and technological advances has thrown us out of balance. Fortunately, we have also been distilling this old wisdom to discard outdated superstitions and myths. Our consciousness has finally evolved into accepting this filtered wisdom of the ages.

We are swimming in a sea of New Age, holistic, and spiritual awareness that seems to have flooded over the dams of old beliefs and of constricted consciousness. The evidence is everywhere. New Thought is becoming mainstream.

The National Institutes of Health is funding studies in acupuncture, herbal medicine, hypnosis, and altered states of consciousness. Insurance companies are covering alternative and complementary healing techniques. Old-line advertising companies are promoting commercial products with international campaigns that feature reincarnation as a selling tool. Movies and television programs trumpet New Age themes to millions of interested viewers.

Why is this happening?

For several hundred years, people have mistakenly believed that technology, once fully developed, would solve the ills of mankind, that science would provide the path out of the woods, away from illness, poverty, misery, and pain.

We now know that technology and science alone are not capable of solving our problems. Technology can be used for good or for bad purposes. Only when used with enlightenment, wisdom, and balance can technology truly help us. We must find the right balance.

Love is the fulcrum of this balance.

When people have intense spiritual experiences, the energy of love is nearly always evoked. This form of love is unconditional, absolute, and transcendent. It is like a pulse of pure energy, an energy that also possesses powerful attributes, such as wisdom, compassion, timelessness, and sublime consciousness. Love is the most basic and pervasive energy that exists. It is the essence of our being and of our universe. Love is the fundamental "building block" of nature connecting and unifying all things, all people.

Love is more than a goal, more than a fuel, more than an ideal. Love is our nature. We *are* love.

I hope that this book will teach you how to recognize love, how to cultivate and enlarge your experience of love (especially toward yourself and in relationships), and how to manifest and radiate your love to others. By doing so, you will inevitably experience more joy, health, and happiness in your life.

Love is the ultimate healer. In the near future some attributes of its energy will indeed be studied scientifically, will be quantified, measured, and understood. Other attributes will remain mysterious, transcendent, and beyond measurement. Fortunately, when the energy of love is deeply felt, its healing effects are experienced, whether or not it is measured or understood.

Physicists know that everything is energy. Nuclear bombs are built based upon techniques of energy transformation and release. Herbal and traditional medicines work because of energy transformations induced at the cellular level. The results are vastly different, but the underlying mechanisms are the same: energy transformations.

The energy of love is potentially more powerful than any bomb and more subtle than any herb. We just have not yet learned how to harness this most basic and pure energy. When we do, healing at *all* levels, individual and planetary, can occur.

Prior to this book, I have been describing the phenomenology, the characteristics of various metaphysical experiences: reincarnation, the nature of the soul, healers and healing, psychic events and mediumistic abilities, the near-death and after-death experiences, and the incredible wisdom of the beings who appear to exist on the "other side."

Now is the opportunity to understand and to experience the energy that is common to and connects all of these experiences, phenomena, and beings. When you do, your life will be expanded and enhanced, and you will be able to remove the blocks and obstacles to your inner peace, joy, and happiness.

Our souls are always drawn toward love. When we truly comprehend the concept that love is an all-encompassing energy whose healing pulse can quickly transform our bodies, minds, and souls, then we will transcend our chronic pain and ills.

How to Use This Book

It is vital to carry your logical, rational mind on this journey. To accept everything without reflection, contemplation, and thoughtfulness would be just as foolish as rejecting everything in the same manner. Science is the art of observing carefully with an unbiased, non-prejudicial eye. I have tried to do that. I have encountered some extremely talented people—psychics, mediums, healers, and others—and I have encountered even more who have limited talent or skill and are mostly opportunists. I have spent many years learning and applying the scientific method, and my skeptical mind is always on alert, passing all my experiences through this scientific filter. But I have also been careful not to throw the baby out with the bathwater. One person or one experience might be disappointing, but the next might be truly extraordinary and should not be discounted because of previous events.

I have written this book to give back a little of that which has been given to me. I pondered how important another book could be. After all, I have already written three, and there is much to digest in those. And spiritual guidance books seem to be everywhere these days. What would another book add?

Teaching is such an individual process, I remembered, dependent on style, timing, personal preferences, values, and so many other factors. Other people, in books or seminars or by example, may tell you similar things, but perhaps in a different way. Even though there may be one truth, many approaches exist to this truth. Yet the answer is always the same; the truth did not change. It does not mean that one teacher is better than the others or that the methods and philosophy of that teacher are superior. Just different, that is all. What works for you is fine, and what does not work for you will work for someone else. We are all going to the same place.

My path to understanding more about our spiritual nature came through many years of arduous academic study, culminating in my medical training, psychiatric specialization, and several decades of post-academic experiences and clinical studies. That has been my path. Others may reach a similar place by having a powerful, spontaneous, and overwhelming experience, such as an NDE (near-death experience). Still others might reach this level using a single technique, such as the practice of meditation, over a longer period of time. These may be their paths. There are many roads to enlightenment. Together we can explore them.

Our beliefs can be altered by the power and immediacy of personal experience. You can begin to understand something when you experience its essence. Your belief becomes a knowing.

It is not enough just to read about the concepts presented here or to rely exclusively on the experiences of others, those presented as examples or illustrations of the concepts. Therefore, throughout this book are exercises and various techniques to enhance your own experiences, to help to transform you directly.

For many years I have advised my patients to keep a dream journal, jotting down memories of dreams as soon as possible after awakening. With a little practice, dream recall is significantly enhanced. And the more details are remembered and recorded, the easier it becomes to analyze the dream accurately. The same is true with meditation and visualization. As you try these exercises, you may find it a useful practice to write down or to journal your thoughts, feelings, observations, and experiences. As with dreams, the more you journal, the easier it becomes for you to remember and to process the details of your experiences.

Practicing these techniques has been difficult for me, so I

can tell you from experience not to get frustrated. Progress may seem quite slow. I find myself getting lazy, not meditating for weeks at a time before I am reminded to resume the practice. I still fall into the ruts and potholes of life, swept away at times by pride or envy or insecurity. We are all human and life is hard. Frustration is a normal and common reaction. We are not a patient species.

As I have mentioned, it is the direction that matters, not the speed. If you are evolving into a more loving, more compassionate, less violent person, then you are moving in the right direction. Like me, you may become distracted, make wrong turns at times, lost until you find the way back. It may seem as if you're taking two steps forward and then one step backwards, but that's all right. That's how it works when we're in human form. Enlightenment is a slow and arduous process, requiring dedication and discipline. It's perfectly fine to rest now and then. You are not really going backwards; you are consolidating and resting.

Progress is not always linear. You may be very advanced when it comes to charity and compassion, but more of a novice concerning anger or patience. It is important not to judge yourself. If you don't judge yourself or allow others to judge you, you will not become frustrated.

The experiences you will encounter as you go through this book are meant to aid your evolution into a loving, joyful, non-violent, and non-fearful being. Since progress along the spiritual path is not linear, you may find some of the concepts and exercises quite easy and others more difficult. This is to be expected.

I have fallen down many times, recovered my awareness, and resumed my journey. You probably have also. With this book, I hope to help you to fall less frequently and to find it easier to recover and to progress. I know that with your letters and feedback to me, you will help me in the same way.

Without the wisdom and inspiration of the Masters, this book would never have been written, for these quotes are stepping-stones to the ideas and practices that are presented in the chapters. The thoughts and concepts contained in the messages are like special seeds that have grown and ripened in my mind over the years into beautiful flowers, and these flowers are now presented to you.

The quotes from the Masters are also like the bells that the Buddhists often sound to remind them to return their wandering minds back to the present time, back to mindfulness and awareness. The messages from the Masters similarly remind us to allow our minds to return to what is important—love, peace, eternal life, spiritual thoughts and practices—and to put aside what is unimportant—material things, pride and ego, violence, fear, worry, and hatred.

The quotes, like the bells, bring us back to awareness. Every time you encounter some words in italics, slow down and digest their meaning. You will rarely taste anything sweeter.

We are all rowing the same boat, and there are ominous storms on the horizon. Violence and shortsightedness seem to dominate our world. We need to row in harmony, to renounce hatred, anger, fear, and pride. We need to have the courage to do the right thing. We need to love and respect one another, to see and appreciate the innate beauty and dignity of everyone, because we are all souls, all of the same substance.

Only by rowing together, as one crew, can we avoid the storms and find our way home.

❦ CHAPTER TWO ❦

The Cycle of Life

We go through so many stages when we're here. We shed a baby body, go into a child's, from child to an adult, an adult into old age. Why shouldn't we go one step beyond and shed the adult body and go onto a spiritual plane? That is what we do. We don't just stop growing; we continue to grow. When we get to the spiritual plane, we keep growing there, too. We go through different stages of development. When we arrive, we're burned out. We have to go through a renewal stage, a learning stage, and a stage of decision. We decide when we want to return, where, and for what reasons. Some choose not to come back. They choose to go on to another stage of development. And they stay in spirit form . . . some for longer than others before they return. It is all growth and learning . . . continuous growth. Our body is just a vehicle for us while we're here. It is our soul and our spirit that last forever.

Our lives are not the result of random actions and events. Lifetimes are wisely and carefully scripted to enhance our learning and evolution.

We choose our parents, who usually are souls with whom we have interacted in prior lifetimes. We learn as children, adolescents, and adults, evolving spiritually as our bodies evolve physically. After our souls leave our bodies at the time of physical "death," our learning continues on higher planes, which are really higher levels of consciousness. We review the lives we have just left, learn our lessons, and plan for our next life. Learning does not end with the death of the body.

There are many levels of consciousness that we visit when our soul departs the physical body. One important level is the learning stage, where we review our lives. We re-experience every encounter, every relationship. We feel the emotions of the people whom we have helped or hurt, loved and hated, or affected positively or negatively. We feel their emotions *very* deeply, because this is a powerful learning device, a sort of instant intense feedback about our behavior while we were on earth, in physical bodies. We learn through relationships, and thus it is important that we understand how we have touched others.

The concept of reincarnation explains and clarifies our present life relationships. Often events in the distant past are still influencing current relationships. Becoming aware of the root causes in prior lives can heal the relationship in the present. Awareness and understanding are powerful healing forces.

I have decided to begin this book with the following example of a regression session because it describes and explains the process of regression therapy that I use, including techniques and interpretations. It is virtually unedited. I want you to experience the sessions as if you were present.

Moreover, this is a fascinating case that involves the present lifetime and also past lives. It illustrates memories from childhood and infancy, and it includes memories from before birth and from after death. It demonstrates the pathways of our souls.

I had been asked by a major television news show to participate in a segment and demonstrate a past-life regression to its vast viewing audience. Hearing about the project and interested in my work, a news reporter for that network volunteered to be the "patient." For this regression, I used the technique known as progressive relaxation, a gentle and gradual descent into the hypnotic state. Hypnosis itself is only a form of focused concentration and relaxation. It is not time travel, and it is not mysterious. In this relaxed and focused state, memory functions are enhanced.

Her session was dramatic, vivid, and intense. She was able to experience childhood, perinatal, and past-life memories, and her life and relationships benefited as a result.

It was a hot, humid day in late May in New York City. The glare and heat emanating from the powerful lights set up for the television taping only added to the sweltering setting. I could feel drops of sweat already forming on my back and under the thin cover of makeup that had been applied to my face. Andrea, the news correspondent, had not yet arrived.

Despite my requests for a relaxed, quiet place, the producers had chosen a downtown apartment as the site of the taping. Instead of a silent room in an air-conditioned studio, we were using a stifling non-air-conditioned apartment. Opening the windows allowed in a slight breeze, but also admitted a cacophony of traffic noises, sirens, and other outside distractions into the already crowded living room. Under these adverse conditions and the added stress of television cameras, I glumly reflected, the chances of a successful regression were greatly diminished.

Finally Andrea arrived. She didn't seem to mind the heat or the sirens sounding beneath us. Apparently, she had grown accustomed to the constant background noises of the city. Andrea was more concerned with the severe menstrual cramps that were wracking her body that afternoon, and I was similarly worried that the pain would prove a serious distraction.

Before the taping, we took a few moments to get acquainted and to discuss the process of hypnosis.

I have included the hypnotic induction in its entirety here, even though parts of it are repetitious, to illustrate this technique and to show you that there is neither magic nor trickery involved in hypnosis and regression. The repetition is deliberate, as it helps to deepen the state that the subject experiences. The dialogue is barely edited because I want you to experience the entire session exactly as it unfolded.

The microphones were turned on, and three cameras stood ready to record the event. Andrea, dressed in a burgundy blouse and dark pants, settled herself on the old well-worn couch. We began the hypnotic induction procedure. Despite her discomfort, Andrea quickly entered into a deep trance state. She later told me her cramps completely disappeared.

In the beginning, she merely listened as I gently instructed her how to reach the deep hypnotic state.

"Here's what we're going to do," I began, "the slower way now. The goal is getting very comfortable, and it's going to be done with your eyes closed. So all you have to do is really follow the directions. Is that okay?"

Andrea nodded yes. She was starting to relax.

"Good. There are faster ways, but I want you to experience the relaxation procedure too. So you're letting your eyes gently close, and the rest of the session will be with your eyes closed. Focus first on your breathing. This is an ancient way for going within; some people call this yoga breathing. The breath is very important. Just imagine, and don't hesitate to use your imagination today, that you can actually breathe out the tensions and stresses in your body, and that you can breathe in the beautiful energy all around you . . . breathing out stress and tension, breathing in beautiful energy. This will help you to go deeper and deeper with each breath. You'll be able to focus on my voice, and let my voice carry you deeper as well.

But let background noises or any other distractions only deepen your level even more. They won't interfere. You can go deep enough today to have wonderful experiences."

I paused for a moment, letting her take a few deepening breaths.

"As we talked about, this is very healthy, for the body and for the mind, to be able to relax, to let go of tension and stress, to just let the body unwind. Good. Your breathing is now very, very comfortable . . . breathing out stress, breathing in beautiful energy. As you do this, relax all of your muscles. You'll be very good at this because you are very aware of your body, but some people are completely unaware. So get yourself as comfortable as you can. You can always move. In case any part of you is uncomfortable, just move it to its most comfortable position. Relax the muscles of your face and your jaw; just feel these muscles relaxing completely. Let go of all tightness and tension in all of these muscles. Relax the muscles of your neck, nice and soft and loose. Lots of people with neck problems or tension headaches have too much tension in their necks, and they're not even aware, so feel your neck completely relaxing. And the muscles of your shoulders, so soft and relaxed. Let go of all tightness and tension. The muscles of your arms—so relaxed now. Let only the couch and the cushions support you. Good; get very, very comfortable."

Her breathing was becoming slower and deeper. I could tell she was already sinking into a deep trance level. I could hear the camera operators behind me scurrying to adjust their positions and moving the heavy television cameras to cover the changing angles as Andrea's head slowly sagged into a very relaxed position.

"And the muscles of your back now, completely relaxing, both the upper back and the lower back, as you go deeper and deeper into this beautiful state of peace. You can let yourself go even deeper with each breath. Now relax the muscles of your stomach and abdomen, so that your breathing stays so peaceful. And finally relax completely the muscles of your legs. Now only the couch is supporting you as you go deeper and deeper into that beautiful state of peace. Very, very good. You'll be able to focus on my voice, and let my voice continue to carry you deeper and deeper, but let the outside noises or distractions only deepen your level even more. You'll hear various noises from time to time, and it won't matter. You can still go very deep.

"And now, imagine or visualize a beautiful light above your head. You can choose the color or colors. Imagine that this is a wonderful healing light, a light of beautiful energy, and a deepening light that will bring you to a deeper and deeper level of peace and serenity. This is also a relaxing light, relaxing you completely. It is a spiritual light, connected to the light above and around you. You pick the color or colors, and let it come into your body now, through the top of your head, illuminating the brain and the spinal cord . . . now flowing down from above to below like a beautiful wave of light, touching every cell and tissue and fiber and organ of your body with peace and love and healing as you go deeper and deeper."

I continued the process of deepening her trance state. My voice had become soft and rhythmic, augmenting the hypnotic effect.

"You'll be able to concentrate on my voice and yet go deeper and deeper as the light fills your heart, healing your heart, and flowing down. Let the light be very powerful, very strong, wherever you need it for healing. As you go deeper and deeper, the rest of the light flows down both legs until it reaches to your feet, filling your body with light, in this beautiful state of peace and relaxation. You are able to focus on my voice. Imagine now that the light is completely surrounding the outside of your body also, as if you are wrapped in a beautiful bubble or cocoon of light, protecting you, healing your skin, deepening your level even more. Now as I count backwards from ten to one, go so deep that your mind is no longer limited by the usual barriers of space or of time, so deep that you can remember everything, every experience that you have ever had, in this body or in any previous body you've had, or even in between bodies, when you've been in a spiritual state. You can remember everything."

Counting down is a very effective deepening technique.

"Ten, nine, eight . . . going deeper and deeper with each number back . . . seven, six, five . . . so deep, so peaceful . . . four, three . . . a beautiful level of serenity and peace . . . two . . . all the anxiety now leaving your body completely . . . one. Good! In this beautiful state of peace, imagine or visualize or feel that you're walking down a beautiful staircase, down, down . . . deeper and deeper . . . down, down . . . each step down deepening your level even more. As you reach the bottom of the steps, in front of you is a beautiful garden, a garden of peace and safety, serenity and love. A wonderful garden. Go into this garden and find a place to rest. Your body, still filled with the light and surrounded by the light, continues to heal, to relax, to recuperate, to rejuvenate. The deepest levels of your mind can open up, and you can remember everything. To show you this, let us begin going back in time, at first a little bit, and then more and more."

Andrea's head was already sinking forward, her chin dangerously approaching the tiny lapel microphone clipped precariously to her burgundy blouse. She was in such a deep level that no further deepening techniques were needed. I decided to begin to travel back in time.

"In a few moments I'll count backward from five to one. Let a childhood memory come to you. If you wish to keep it a pleasant memory, that's all right, or it can be a memory that teaches you something or that has some value in helping you to feel more joy or peace or happiness in your life now. Let yourself remember completely, with feelings, with sensations, using all of your senses. If you ever feel uncomfortable, you can always detach from it and float above the scene or the memory. You can float and watch from a distance. But if you're not uncomfortable, stay with the memory and remember it vividly. You'll be able to talk from that deep state and yet stay in a deep, deep level and continue to experience. But now as I count backwards, let the memory focus in vivid detail, using all of your senses. A childhood memory. Five, four . . . you can remember everything . . . three . . . focus now . . . two . . . it's all there . . . one. Be there! For a few moments, re-experience this, remember it. You'll be able to talk and tell me what you're experiencing, and yet continue to stay in a deep, deep level, continuing to experience. What do you remember? What comes to you?"

"It's winter," Andrea began. "My dad and I are taking a walk in our neighborhood. He always asked me to go for these winter walks. We're with our dog, a husky, and the wind is *really* blowing, and it's snowy, and we're walking into the wind, and I love it because it's time for just my dad and me, and none of the other kids ever get asked to go. And it's freezing cold, and my dad wears this wonderful parka he always wore, and the moon's out, and our dog loves the snow." Andrea's voice was more child-like. A strong Midwestern accent had replaced the polished cadence of a professional journalist. "We walk, and we talk, and we kick snow up and it's nighttime so nobody's out driving and we're walking in the middle of the street. The lampposts are those old lampposts with those big globe lights, and it's beautiful. It's like the whole world has stopped and it's just my dad and me." A radiant smile filled her face, which seemed softer and more vulnerable.

"Can you see yourself?" I asked. "What do you look like? What are you wearing?"

"I had a terrible haircut," she observed. She seemed surprised.

"How old are you?" I inquired, trying to anchor her in the scene.

"Eight."

"And you have your coat on, too, of course."

"I can't see what color it is," she hesitantly replied. "I can't tell. I've got a scarf on, and mittens, and boots, but my feet aren't warm."

"And your dad's coat, what is that like?"

"It's a red parka, and it has a shell of white wool. He bought it in Chicago, and he always wears it in the winter. It has a hood that has fur around it. It's like what my dad always wears."

"This seems like a very happy time for you because you're with your dad and your dog and it's so peaceful."

I observed some tears at the corners of her eyes. "Is there sadness with this memory?"

Andrea shook her head no.

"Just happy?"

She smiled her answer.

"It just makes me wish I were a little girl again," she softly added.

"Well, right now you can be," I explained. "Just experience it. It's vivid; you can be right there in the snow. You can even, if you want, hear the crunching of the snow and see your dog playing in the snow, loving it. You can feel without being uncomfortable." I wanted Andrea to experience this beautiful childhood memory fully, to use all of her senses and feelings.

"We never went home early," she continued. "We would take long, long walks. He never . . . there's no rushing. It's up the street and then I can't see where we are going but we always come back to the same spot, and we go home, and my mom has hot chocolate." Another shining smile softened her face.

I became aware of the whirring of the television cameras. I decided to summarize her experience and to move on to even deeper levels. Because of the time constraints of filming, I had to be more directive in making connections and interpretations than I am with a patient in my office. I was also concerned that others were in the room who ought not be privy to personal information; thus, there were certain memories that I allowed Andrea to experience in silence. Additionally, this was intended to be a demonstration and not a therapeutic session.

"That's nice. What I would like for you to do is to remember the love and the caring that is there at this time, between you and your father, and you and your mother. Because having that hot chocolate there is very compassionate and loving, too. These are wonderful memories of love and of youth and of compassion, of your mother and your father, and the closeness that is there with your father, and these special walks. And so even after you're awake, you'll remember the love, the compassion, the caring. This is a wonderful memory, and you'll take it back with you . . . the goodness, the happiness, the joy, and even with the dog, everything, just the happiness of it. Life is meant to be that way. There are so many opportunities to love, to be compassionate. It can be very simple—a walk with your father; it doesn't have to be expensive. A walk with your father on a winter night, and your dog, and your mother having the chocolate there. You'll remember this even after you're awake. Are you ready to go farther back now?"

"Yes," she answered without any hesitation. Andrea had tasted the sweetness and the intensity of these memories, and she wanted more.

"Good. Just float above that memory. Float above, feeling so free and so light, floating above now, leaving that time, letting that memory fade away. Now we're going to go even farther back, back before you were born, in utero, in your mother's womb. Once again I'll count backwards from five to one, and whatever comes to you, whatever comes into your awareness, is fine. Don't judge it or critique it or analyze it, just experience. This is all for the experience. As I reach one, be there, before you were born, in utero, and see if you feel or sense any feelings, thoughts, or sensations, whether they are physical or emotional or even spiritual. Perhaps you will discover why you are choosing this life and these parents. Whatever comes to you is fine. You may become aware of events happening outside of the body. This happens sometimes, too. It does not matter. Whatever you experience is fine. Is that okay?"

Andrea slowly nodded her assent.

"Good. Take a beautiful breath or two and go even deeper, in that deep, deep level again. As I count backwards from five to one, we'll go back before you were born, in this life, in utero. We'll see what you can remember and experience. Five, you can remember everything . . . four, going back before you were born, in utero, in your mother's womb . . . three, whatever comes into your awareness is okay . . . two, coming into focus now . . . one. Be there. Spend a few moments in that environment, becoming aware of anything . . . sensations, physical, emotional, spiritual . . . any impressions or thoughts. Sometimes you can even become aware of your mother's feelings or thoughts because you're so closely bonded. Or even of your father, who is close by. Spend a few moments remembering that, re-experiencing that. Now once again, you'll be able to talk and still stay in a deep, deep state in a deep level and continue to experience. You'll be able to tell me what you are experiencing."

"What do you become aware of?" I asked.

Andrea responded with a quick smile, and I immediately

knew she had successfully bridged years of time. She had emerged at the very beginnings of her present life.

"My mom's real happy," she said simply. Her smile never faded.

"Good, good," I answered, relieved that she was remembering something important. The cameras were recording everything. "You can feel her happiness?"

She nodded yes.

"Good. So you're really wanted. This is important. What else? What else do you become aware of? How do you feel?"

"I can't tell."

"Any other impressions or sensations?"

"My mom has a funny haircut." Even before her birth Andrea was able to observe and evaluate hairstyles.

"Yes, you can see that. How would you describe the haircut? Funny in what way?"

"Looks like she took a razor and cut it herself. It's real short. My dad likes it that way." She was also aware of her father's feelings, his likes and dislikes.

"He likes it short like that?"

"Yes. He's real handsome," she added.

"You can see him too, looking younger now? Good. I'm very glad that you're wanted; they're happy. This is a good environment to come into."

"They're *very* excited." Andrea was content to remain in that place, to enjoy once again these wonderful feelings. She did not care at all that time was passing or that tape was rolling.

"Good. Then let's go through the birth, as I count to three, without any pain or discomfort, just observing it, to see what you become aware of through the birth experience. On the count of three but with no pain or discomfort to you. One, two, three. Go through it. Whatever you become aware of is fine. What do you experience?"

Andrea remained silent for ten or fifteen seconds. Finally she answered.

"Dark places."

"How do you feel now?" I did not know where she was, what these "dark places" were.

"Like it's not over," she explained. Now I understood.

"Oh, you're not finished being born. Okay, you can go through it, no pain, no discomfort. Go through, be born now."

"My mother didn't take any anesthetic. She didn't. I come out pink." This was an interesting observation for a newborn.

"Pink, yes. And you're . . . ?"

"Crying, but I'm fine. My mom's fine."

"She didn't want the anesthetic?"

"She refused it. She didn't want me to be born blue like the other babies." Sometimes a general anesthetic administered during labor can affect the baby.

"I understand. And you weren't; you were pink, alert, crying. Can you see her now? What do you see?"

Andrea began to laugh out loud. Waves of amused laughter burst from her. "Everybody's happy. She's put in a room with other moms. My dad's a doctor but she doesn't get her own room." There was irony in her observation.

"It's blue outside," she added. "It's a sunny day."

"You're aware of many things," I noted. "Many details. Do they bring you to her? Is that how it works?"

"She just had me in her arms. It's like I don't leave her."

"This is the part you remember, the part with her. She's doing okay with you?"

"She's having fun. She's skinny, didn't put on much weight." Andrea paid a great deal of attention to physical features, such as haircuts and weight.

"But you're okay?" I asked.

"I'm *fine*," she reassured me.

"That's a good memory. You're aware of so many details now. Just let it soak in, being in her arms, how she looks with this short haircut and everything. Didn't put on much weight. And you're happy to be there. Good."

"My dad's so proud he won't shut up. He's bugging everybody."

"Is he bringing people in with him?"

"He won't stop. He's so obnoxious. He's pulling everybody in the hospital to a window to see, to take a look at me. He's so obnoxious. He's funny."

"He's connected to you very strongly, right from the beginning," I remarked, remembering their loving connection while walking on a winter's night eight years later, "but it's a loving obnoxious. Very good. Well, once again you will remember that even after you're awake. I know there are lots more details. You don't have to tell me about all of these details now. There's so much more that you can see and become aware of and describe. Everything—colors, the outside, the room, the other babies, what your dad's wearing, what he looks like—the whole thing. Just become aware of it. Soak up the love, even if he's obnoxious; it's all love, and that's very good. He maintained that love; that was wonderful. There's a great deal of happiness and joy. It's wonderful to be received into the world this way, wanted, with joy, with happiness, with love. You'll remember even more details. Let yourself soak them up, even more details, of the room, of the size, how it's arranged. But the most important of all is the love."

Andrea's face darkened. "The woman in the bed next to my mother—her husband just came in. She just had a baby and he wants to have sex with her."

"In that room?" I questioned, surprised at the sudden clarity of this unpleasant memory.

"Yeah, and she says no. He's not very nice. My mother's not happy."

"Did she know about this?"

"Yeah, there're curtains between each bed, but this man is very vulgar."

"But his wife refused."

"Yeah—she just had a *baby*!" Andrea emphatically explained.

"I know."

"My mother's not happy," she repeated.

"Does he leave?"

"No."

Some moments of silence followed. I filled the void.

"He's not very understanding. You can see the family you were born into is not only much more understanding, but there's so much more for you, too, to look forward to, because there's compassion, there's understanding."

"My neck is heavy," Andrea exclaimed as her head fell onto the arm of the couch. Again I could hear the television equipment being moved to adjust to her new reclining position.

"Good. Getting very comfortable now. Are you ready to leave that scene?" She didn't answer, so I let her linger there for a few more moments.

"Or do you want to stay there a little bit longer? Why don't you stay there longer and really go deep. Let your breathing go deep. Your neck is perfect now. You'll be able to rest very comfortably there, and focus on the happiness and any more details that come to you, like the person in the other bed. Don't let that affect you in any negative way. That wasn't your family. Experience that a little more, and then see the connection to when you were older in the snow."

I decided to make some connections for her.

"The proud father, your father, so proud when you were born, and then these loving walks in the winter. It's all part of the same love, the same connection. What difference is seven or eight years? This doesn't mean anything. The love never stops; it's forever. Just see the connections there and spend some time in this state, because this is a very good state to be in, with happy memories. You've been able to take this love that was there from before you were born, because you were aware, even before you were born, of the love that was there, the happiness of your mother, the happiness of your father. You can see all the connections throughout your life, and you are able to bring that love and not only to receive it, but you've been able to give it back to others, ones that you've loved." Andrea was smiling again, soaking up these thoughts.

"So this has been not only fortunate, you earned this, you deserve this, and there's nothing more important than love. Now we're ready to go farther back. Is that okay?" Now she agreed.

"Good. So just float above this scene now, leave the hospital and the nursery, float above it, and let the scene gently fade away. Imagine now that there's a beautiful door in front of you, and this is a door into past lifetimes or into spiritual states, because these are important also, and they may shed some light onto why there's so much love in your life now or on a particular person or symptom or whatever you would like to focus on. When you go through the door as I count backwards from five to one, you'll see a beautiful light on the other side of the door."

"I can already see it coming through the door around the cracks," Andrea commented. She was in a profoundly deep trance level.

"You can already see the light? Good. Well, then we'll go through the door. There'll be a scene there. It may be from an ancient time; it may be a past life. Join the scene, join it, go through the door and into the beautiful light as I count backwards. Five, the door opens. It pulls you; it attracts you. There is something for you to learn on the other side of this door. Four, you step through the door and into the beautiful light. Three, moving through the light, you become aware of a scene or person or figure on the other side of the light. Let it come into complete focus as I reach the number one. Two, coming into focus now; you can remember everything. One. Be there! If you find yourself in a body, look down at your feet and see what kind of footwear you have on, whether shoes or sandals or boots or furs or perhaps nothing at all. Look at your clothes, paying attention to any details. Feel textures, because it's not just seeing but also feeling. Any of your senses."

"I'm wearing men's boots," she observed.

"Men's boots?" I repeated.

"I don't have any for myself. But I'm not a man, I'm a girl. But I don't have boots for a girl because we can't afford it."

"You can't afford it so you're wearing men's boots instead?"

"Boys' boots," she corrected. "They're like with round toes, and I'm embarrassed because I shouldn't be wearing these boots."

"Because of the boy thing?"

"Yeah, girls' . . . I mean, I should have worn girls' boots, but somehow . . ."

"What about the rest of your clothes?"

"I have a skirt on, and it's down to the ground. It's dark red with an apron or an embroidery or something on the front part. It's like there's an extra piece of cloth. I have a bonnet." Andrea's eyes were fluttering under her closed eyelids as she scanned her clothes.

"A bonnet, yes. And about how old are you?"

"Nine or ten."

"Okay. Are there others there around you? Anybody else that you become aware of? A home, a house?" I wanted to elicit even more details from that time.

"A sod house. We live in the prairie somewhere. But I don't see anybody else's house there. It's just my house. And my boots are my . . . I have an older brother, and these are his boots. They're the ones I wear now. It's in the plains somewhere. It's west, but it's not Rocky Mountains west. We're in the plains. We're farmers." Andrea was remembering a previous life in the American Midwest.

"Kind of eking it out there," I added.

"We have a cow, and we have a garden. There's a well and the house is real simple."

"Good. Now I want you to become aware of your parents, too, not just your brother. I'll count to three. See the whole family who lives there. One, two, three. The whole family, maybe dinnertime or sometime. Let yourself become aware of the others now."

"Everybody's standing out front of the house like they're getting their picture taken. Because they are; they're standing like a picture postcard."

"Good. You can see them now."

"Except it's my same mom and dad. Same eyes." Usually we reincarnate in different relationships, but in this life on the plains, Andrea's parents apparently were the same as in her current life.

"Sometimes it works out that way. We come around again and again with our loved ones. It often works that way. Your brother, do you see him?"

"I have only one brother, and he's littler. But I don't think I know him."

"You don't recognize him?"

"I can't even see his face," Andrea explained.

"Are his the boots that you have?" I was confused because I thought she had said that the boots were from her older brother.

"No. There was another brother, but he's not there. He's not the right brother."

"For the boots?" I asked, looking for clarification.

"Not the right brother for the boots. I got my boots from my other brother, but he's not there."